By the same author

Just For You
Heart Gifts
Lovingly
Prayerfully
Somebody Loves You
Loving Promises
Loving Thoughts
And The Greatest Of These Is Love
Remembering With Love

THANKFULLY

Helen Steiner Rice

THANKFULLY

Including The Christmas Guest and other poems

Decorations by Biro

Hutchinson

London Sydney Auckland Johannesburg

© Fleming H. Revell 1971
© This arrangement including decorations
Hutchinson & Co. (Publishers) Ltd 1975

First published 1975
Reprinted March 1977
Reprinted March 1978
Reprinted June 1980
Reprinted September 1982
Reprinted January 1990

This edition published in 1986 by Hutchinson Ltd
Reprinted 1989

An imprint of Century Hutchinson Ltd
Brookmount House, 62-65 Chandos Place,
Covent Garden, London WC2N 4NW

Century Hutchinson Australia (Pty) Ltd
89-91 Albion Street, Surry Hills, New South Wales 2010

Century Hutchinson Group (NZ) Ltd
32-34 View Road, PO Box 40-086, Glenfield, Auckland 10

Century Hutchinson Group (SA) (Pty) Ltd
PO Box 337, Bergvlei 2012, South Africa

Printed and bound in Great Britain by
Scotprint Limited, Musselburgh.

ISBN 0 09 121730 X

Contents

Unaware, we pass 'Him' by

On life's busy thoroughfares
We meet with *Angels* unawares –
But we are too busy to listen or hear,
Too busy to sense that God is near,
Too busy to stop and recognize
The grief that lies in another's eyes,
Too busy to offer to help or share,
Too busy to sympathize or care,
Too busy to do the *Good Things* we should,
Telling ourselves we would if we could . . .
But life is too swift and the pace is too great
And we dare not pause for we might be late
For our next appointment which means so much,
We are willing to brush off the Saviour's touch
And we tell ourselves there will come a day
We will have more time to pause on our way . . .
But before we know it 'life's sun has set'
And we've passed the Saviour but never met,
For hurrying along life's thoroughfare
We passed Him by and remained unaware
That within the *Very Sight of Our Eye*,
Unnoticed, the Son of God Passed By.

Foreword to the Christmas Guest

This Lovely Legend
is centuries old,
repeated, rewritten,
Revised and *Retold* . . .
And through countless ages
this story survives
As Christmas rekindles,
renews and revives
Man's longing to look
in the dear Lord's face
And bask in the warmth
of His love and His grace,
Not knowing each day
that He comes disguised
And begs to be welcomed
and recognized . . .
But unperceivingly
we turn *Him* away,
Not expecting '*This Guest*'
on a routine day . . .
But the '*Shoeless Beggar*'
and the '*Bent Old Crone*'
And the '*Homeless Child*'
so lost and alone
Come daily and knock at
'*The Door of Our Heart*'
But we are too busy,
and unseen '*They*' depart . . .
And man goes on searching
year after year
Hoping that someday
The Lord will appear!

The Christmas Guest

as retold by Helen Steiner Rice

When I was a child I loved to hear
This story my Grandma told each year,
She told it in her native tongue,
And I was very, very young . . .
But yet this story seemed to be
Filled with wonderment for me,
For in my childish heart there grew
The dream that I might see Him, too,
For He might call on me this way
So I must watch for Him each day . . .
And that is why 'The Christmas Guest'
Is still the story I love best –
And I retell it to you now,
For I can't help but feel somehow
That children Everywhere should hear
The story Grandma told each year . . .
For Christmas Day is doubly blest
When Jesus is Our Christmas Guest!

It happened one day
at the year's white end,
Two neighbours called
on an old-time friend
And they found his shop
so meagre and mean,
Made gay with a thousand
boughs of green,

And Conrad was sitting
with face a-shine
When he suddenly stopped
as he stitched a twine

And said, 'Old friends,
at dawn today,
When the cock was crowing
the night away,
The Lord appeared
in a dream to me
And said, "I am coming
your guest to be" . . .

So I've been busy
with feet astir,
Strewing my shop
with branches of fir. The table is spread
and the kettle is shined
And over the rafters
the holly is twined,

And now I will wait
for my Lord to appear
And listen closely
so I will hear

His step as He nears
my humble place
And I open the door
and look in His face' . . .

So his friends went home
and left Conrad alone,
For this was the happiest
day he had known,
For, long since, his family
has passed away
And Conrad had spent
a sad Christmas Day . . .

But he knew with the Lord
as his Christmas guest
This Christmas would be
the dearest and best,

And he listened with only
joy in his heart,
And with every sound
he would rise with a start
And look for the Lord
to be standing there
In answer to
his earnest prayer . . .

So he ran to the window
after hearing a sound,
But all that he saw
on the snow-covered ground
Was a shabby beggar
whose shoes were torn
And all of his clothes
were ragged and worn . . .

So Conrad was touched
and went to the door
And he said, 'Your feet
must be frozen and sore,
And I have some shoes
in my shop for you
And a coat that will keep
you warmer, too . . . '

So with grateful heart
the man went away,
But as Conrad noticed
the time of day
He wondered what made
the dear Lord so late
And how much longer he'd have to wait,

When he heard a knock
and ran to the door,
But it was only
a stranger once more,
A bent, old crone
with a shawl of black,
A bundle of faggots
piled on her back.

She asked for only
a place to rest,
But that was reserved
for Conrad's Great Guest . . .
But her voice seemed to plead,
'Don't send me away,
Let me rest for awhile
on Christmas Day,'

So Conrad brewed her
a steaming cup
And told her to sit
at the table and sup . . .

But after she left
he was filled with dismay
For he saw that the hours
were passing away
And the Lord had not come
as He said He would,
And Conrad felt sure
he had misunderstood . . .

When out of the stillness
he heard a cry,
'Please help me
and tell me where am I,'

So again he opened
his friendly door
And stood disappointed
as twice before.

It was only a child
who had wandered away
And was lost from her family
on Christmas Day . . .

Again Conrad's heart
was heavy and sad,
But he knew he should make
this little child glad,
So he called her in
and wiped her tears
And quieted all
her childish fears . . .

Then he led her back
to her home once more
But as he entered
his own darkened door
He knew that the Lord
was not coming today
For the hours of Christmas
had passed away . . .
So he went to his room
and knelt down to pray
And he said, 'Dear Lord,
why did You delay,
What kept You from coming
to call on me,
For I wanted so much
Your face to see' . . .

When soft in the silence
a voice he heard
'Lift up your head
for I kept My word –
Three times My shadow
crossed your floor –
Three times I came
to your lonely door –

For I was the beggar
with bruised, cold feet,
I was the woman
you gave to eat,
And I was the child
on the homeless street.'

Be of Good Cheer –
There's Nothing to Fear!

Cheerful thoughts like sunbeams
Lighten up the 'darkest fears'
For when the heart is happy
There's just no time for tears –
And when the face is smiling
It's impossible to frown,
And when you are 'high-spirited'
You cannot feel 'low-down' –
For the nature of our attitude
Toward circumstantial things
Determines our acceptance
Of the problems that life brings,
And since fear and dread and worry
Cannot help in any way,
It's much healthier and happier
To be cheerful every day –
And if you'll only try it
You will find, without a doubt,
A cheerful attitude's something
No one should be without –
For when the heart is cheerful
It cannot be filled with fear,
And without fear the way ahead
Seems more distinct and clear –
And we realize there's nothing
We need ever face alone
For our *Heavenly Father* loves us
And our problems are His own.

It's a Wonderful World

In spite of the fact
we complain and lament
And view this old world
with much discontent,
Deploring conditions
and grumbling because
There's so much injustice
and so many flaws,
It's a wonderful world
and it's people like you
Who make it that way
by the things that they do –
For a warm, ready smile
or a kind, thoughtful deed,
Or a hand outstretched
in an hour of need
Can change our whole outlook
and make the world bright
Where a minute before
just nothing seemed right –
It's a *Wonderful World*
and it always will be
If we keep our eyes open
and focused to see
The *Wonderful Things*
man is capable of
When he opens his heart
to *God* and *His Love*.

We Can't . . . but God Can!

Why things happen as they do
We do not always know,
And we cannot always fathom
Why our spirits sink so low . . .
We flounder in our dark distress,
We are wavering and unstable,
But when we're most inadequate
The Lord God's *Always Able* . . .
For though we are incapable,
God's powerful and great,
And there's no darkness of the mind
That God can't penetrate . . .
And all that is required of us
Whenever things go wrong
Is to trust in God implicitly
With a *Faith* that's deep and strong,
And while He may not instantly
Unravel all the strands
Of the tangled thoughts that trouble us –
He completely understands . . .
And in His time, if we have *Faith*,
He will gradually restore
The brightness to our spirit
That we've been longing for . . .
So remember, there's no cloud too dark
For God's light to penetrate
If we keep on believing
And have *Faith Enough* to *Wait!*

Spring Awakens What Autumn Puts to Sleep

A garden of asters of varying hues,
Crimson-pinks and violet-blues,
Blossoming in the hazy Fall
Wrapped in Autumn's lazy pall –
But early frost stole in one night
And like a chilling, killing blight
It touched each pretty aster's head
And now the garden's still and dead
And all the lovely flowers that bloomed
Will soon be buried and entombed
In Winter's icy shroud of snow
But oh, how wonderful to know
That after Winter comes the Spring
To breathe new life in everything,
And all the flowers that fell in death
Will be awakened by Spring's breath –
For in God's Plan both men and flowers
Can only reach 'bright shining hours'
By dying first to rise in glory
And prove again the Easter Story.

Beyond Our Asking

More than hearts can imagine
or minds comprehend,
God's bountiful gifts
are ours without end –
We ask for a cupful
when the vast sea is ours,
We pick a small rosebud
from a garden of flowers,
We reach for a sunbeam
but the sun still abides,
We draw one short breath
but there's air on all sides –
Whatever we ask for
falls short of God's giving
For *His Greatness* exceeds
every facet of living,
And always God's ready
and eager and willing
To pour out His mercy
completely fulfilling
All of man's needs
for peace, joy and rest
For God gives His children
Whatever is Best –
Just give Him a chance
to open *His Treasures*
And He'll fill your life
with unfathomable pleasures,
Pleasures that never
grow worn-out and faded
And leave us depleted,
disillusioned and jaded –

For God has a 'storehouse'
just filled to the brim
With all that man needs
if we'll only ask Him.

What More Can You Ask

God's love endureth forever –
What a wonderful thing to know
When the tides of life run against you
And your spirit is downcast and low . . .
God's kindness is ever around you,
Always ready to freely impart
Strength to your faltering spirit,
Cheer to your lonely heart . . .
God's presence is ever beside you,
As near as the reach of your hand,
You have but to tell Him your troubles,
There is nothing He won't understand . . .
And knowing God's love is unfailing,
And His mercy unending and great,
You have but to trust in His promise –
'God comes not too soon or too late' . . .
So wait with a heart that is patient
For the goodness of God to prevail –
For never do prayers go unanswered,
And His mercy and love never fail.

'I Am the Way, The Truth and the Life'

I Am the Way
so just follow *Me*
Though the way be rough
and you cannot see . . .

I Am the Truth
which all men seek
So heed not 'false prophets'
nor the words that they speak . . .

I Am the Life
and I hold the key
That opens the door
to *Eternity* . . .

And in this dark world
I Am the Light
To the Promised Land
Where There is No Night!

Let Go and Let God!

When you're troubled and worried and sick at heart
And your plans are upset and your world falls apart,
Remember God's ready and waiting to share
The burden you find much too heavy to bear –
So with faith, '*Let Go*' and '*Let God*' lead the way
Into a brighter and less troubled day.

Look on the Sunny Side

There are always two sides,
the *Good* and the *Bad*,
The *Dark* and the *Light*,
the *Sad* and the *Glad* –
But in looking back over
the *Good* and the *Bad*
We're aware of the number
of *Good Things* we've had –
And in counting our blessings
we find when we're through
We've no reason at all
to complain or be blue –
So thank God for *Good* things
He has already done,
And be grateful to Him
for the battles you've won,
And know that the same God
who helped you before
Is ready and willing
to help you once more –
Then with faith in your heart
reach out for God's Hand
And accept what He sends,
though you can't understand –
For *Our Father* in heaven
always knows what is best,
And if you trust in His wisdom
your life will be blest,
For always remember
that whatever betide you,
You are never alone
for God is beside you.

Things to Be Thankful For

The good, green earth beneath our feet,
The air we breathe, the food we eat,
Some work to do, a goal to win,
A hidden longing deep within
That spurs us on to bigger things
And helps us meet what each day brings,
All these things and many more
Are things we should be thankful for . . .
And most of all our thankful prayers
Should rise to God because He cares!

Death is Only a Part of Life

We enter this world
from '*The Great Unknown*'
And *God* gives each *Spirit*
a form of its own
And endows this form
with a heart and a soul
To spur man on
to his ultimate goal . . .
For all men are born
to *Return* as they *Came*
And birth and death
are in essence the same
And man is but born
to die and arise
For beyond this world
in beauty there lies
The purpose of death

24

which is but to gain
Life Everlasting
in *God's Great Domain* . . .
And no one need make
this journey alone
For *God* has promised
to take care of *His* own.

On the Other Side of Death

Death is a *Gateway*
we all must pass through
To reach that Fair Land
where the soul's born anew,
For man's born to die
and his sojourn on earth
Is a short span of years
beginning with birth . . .
And like pilgrims we wander
until death takes our hand
And we start on our journey
to God's Promised Land,
A place where we'll find
no suffering nor tears,
Where *Time* is not counted
by days, months or years . . .
And in this Fair City
that God has prepared
Are unending joys
to be happily shared
With all of our loved ones
who patiently wait
On Death's Other Side
to open '*The Gate*'!

There Are Blessings in Everything

Blessings come in many guises
That God alone in love devises,
And sickness which we dread so much
Can bring a very 'healing touch' –
For often on the 'wings of pain'
The peace we sought before in vain
Will come to us with 'sweet surprise'
For God is merciful and wise –
And through long hours of tribulation
God gives us time for meditation,
And no sickness can be counted loss
That teaches us to 'bear our cross.'

Brighten the Corner Where You Are

We cannot all be famous
or be listed in '*Who's Who*,'
But every person great or small
has important work to do,
For seldom do we realize
the importance of small deeds
Or to what degree of greatness
unnoticed kindness leads –
For it's not the big celebrity
in a world of fame and praise,
But it's doing unpretentiously
in undistinguished ways
The work that God assigned to us,
unimportant as it seems,
That makes our task outstanding
and brings reality to dreams –
So do not sit and idly wish
for wider, new dimensions
Where you can put in practice
your many '*Good Intentions*' –
But at the spot God placed you
begin at once to do
Little things to brighten up
the lives surrounding you,
For if everybody brightened up
the spot on which they're standing
By being more considerate
and a little less demanding,
This dark old world would very soon
eclipse the 'Evening Star'
If everybody *Brightened Up*
the Corner Where They Are !

Everyone Needs Someone

People need people
and friends need friends,
And we all need love
for a full life depends
Not on vast riches
or great acclaim,
Not on success
or on worldly fame,
But just in knowing
that someone cares
And holds us close
in their thoughts and prayers –
For only the knowledge
that we're understood
Makes everyday living
feel *Wonderfully Good*,
And we rob ourselves
of life's greatest need
When we 'lock up our hearts'
and fail to heed
The outstretched hand
reaching to find
A kindred spirit
whose heart and mind
are lonely and longing
to somehow share
Our joys and sorrows
and to make us aware
That life's completeness
and richness depends
On the things we share
with our loved ones and friends.

A Friend Is a Gift of God

Among the great and glorious gifts
our heavenly Father sends
Is the *Gift* of *Understanding*
that we find in loving friends,
For in this world of trouble
that is filled with anxious care
Everybody needs a friend
in whom they're free to share
The little secret heartaches
that lay heavy on their mind,
Not just a mere acquaintance
but someone who's '*Just Our Kind*' –
For, somehow, in the generous heart
of loving, faithful friends
The good God in His charity
and wisdom always sends
A sense of understanding
and the power of perception
And mixes these fine qualities
with kindness and affection
So when we need some sympathy
or a friendly hand to touch,
Or an ear that listens tenderly
and speaks words that mean so much,
We seek our true and trusted friend
in the knowledge that we'll find
A heart that's sympathetic
and an understanding mind. . . .
And often just without a word
there seems to be a union
Of thoughts and kindred feelings
for *God* gives *True Friends* communion.

When Two People Marry

Your hearts are filled with happiness
so great and overflowing,
You cannot comprehend it
for it's far beyond all knowing
How any heart could hold such joy
or feel the fullness of
The wonder and the glory
and the ecstasy of love –
You wish that you could capture it
and never let it go
So you might walk forever
in its radiant magic glow . . .
But love in all its ecstasy
is such a fragile thing,
Like gossamer in cloudless skies
or a hummingbird's small wing,
But love that lasts *Forever*
must be made of something strong,
The kind of strength that's gathered
when the heart can hear no song –
When the 'sunshine' of your wedding day
runs into 'stormy weather'

And hand in hand you brave the gale
and climb steep hills together,
And clinging to each other
while the thunder rolls above
You seek divine protection
in *Faith* and *Hope* and *Love* . . .
For '*Days of Wine and Roses*'
never make love's dream come true,
It takes sacrifice and teardrops,
and problems shared by two,
To give true love its *Beauty*,
its *Grandeur* and its *Fineness*
And to mold an 'earthly ecstasy'
into *Heavenly Divineness*.

The Gift of Friendship

Friendship is a *Priceless Gift*
that cannot be bought or sold,
But its value is far greater
than a mountain made of gold –
For gold is cold and lifeless,
it can neither see nor hear,
And in the time of trouble
it is powerless to cheer –
It has no ears to listen,
no heart to understand,
It cannot bring you comfort
or reach out a helping hand –
So when you ask God for a *Gift*,
be thankful if *He* sends
Not diamonds, pearls or riches,
but the love of real true friends.

Love One Another for Love Is of God

Every couple should remember
that what the world calls love
Is not something man invented,
but it comes from God above . . .
And love can be neglected
and oftentimes abused,
Perverted and distorted,
misguided and misused,
Or it can be developed
by living every day
Near to God, *Our Father*,
and following in *His Way* . . .
For God alone can teach you
the meaning of true love,
And He can help establish
the life you're dreaming of
In which you live together
in happiness and peace,
Enjoying married blessings
that day by day increase . . .
For love that is immortal
has its source in God above,
And the love you give each other
is founded on His love . . .
And though upon *Your Wedding Day*
it seems *Yours* and *Yours Alone*,
If you but ask, God takes *Your Love*
and blends it with *His Own*.

A Child's Faith

'Jesus loves me, this I know,
For the *Bible* tells me so' –
Little children ask no more,
For love is all they're looking for,
And in a small child's shining eyes
The *Faith* of all the ages lies
And tiny hands and tousled heads
That kneel in prayer by little beds
Are close to the dear Lord's heart
And of His Kingdom more a part
Than we who search, and never find,
The answers to our questioning mind
For *Faith* in things we cannot see
Requires a child's simplicity
For, lost in life's complexities,
We drift upon uncharted seas
And slowly *Faith* disintegrates
While wealth and power accumulates –
And the more man learns, the less he knows,
And the more involved his thinking grows
And, in his arrogance and pride,
No longer is man satisfied
To place his confidence and love
With childlike *Faith* in God above –
Oh, Father, grant once more to men
A simple childlike *Faith* again
And, with a small child's trusting eyes,
May all men come to realize
That *Faith* alone can save man's soul
And lead him to a *Higher Goal.*

Life's Golden Autumn

Birthdays come and *Birthdays* go
and with them comes the thought
Of all the happy *Memories*
that the passing years have brought –
And looking back across the years
it's a joy to reminisce,
For *Memory Opens Wide the Door*
on a happy day like this,
And with a sweet nostalgia
we longingly recall
The *Happy Days of Long Ago*
that seem the *Best of All* –
But *Time* cannot be halted
in its swift and endless flight
And *Age* is sure to follow *Youth*
as *Day* comes after *Night* –
And once again it's proven
that the restless brain of man
Is powerless to alter
God's Great Unchanging Plan –
But while our step grows slower
and we grow more tired, too,
The *Soul* goes soaring *Upward*
to realms untouched and new,
For growing older only means
the *Spirit* grows serene
And we behold things with *Our Souls*
that our eyes have never seen –
And *Birthdays* are but *Gateways*
to *Eternal Life Above*
Where 'God's children' live *Forever*
in the *Beauty* of *His Love*.

Death Is a Doorway

On the '*Wings* of *Death*'
the '*Soul* takes *Flight*'
Into the land where
'*There is No Night*' –
For those who believe
what the Saviour said
Will rise in glory
though they be dead . . .
So death comes to us
just to '*Open the Door*'
To the *Kingdom of God*
and *Life Evermore*.

Dark Shadows Fall in the Lives of Us All

Sickness and sorrow come to us all,
But through it we grow and learn to 'stand tall' –
For trouble is 'part and parcel of life'
And no man can grow without struggle and strife,
And the more we endure with patience and grace
The stronger we grow and the more we can face –
And the more we can face, the greater our love,
And with love in our hearts we are more conscious of
The pain and the sorrow in lives everywhere,
So it is through trouble that we learn how to share.

What Is Marriage?

Marriage is the union
of two people in love,
And love is sheer magic
for it's woven of
Gossamer dreams,
enchantingly real,
That people in love
are privileged to feel –
But the 'exquisite ecstasy'
that captures the heart
Of two people in love
is just a small part
Of the beauty and wonder
and *Miracle* of
The growth and fulfilment
and evolvement of love –

For only long years
of living together
And sharing and caring
in all kinds of weather
Both pleasure and pain,
the glad and the sad,
Teardrops and laughter,
the good and the bad,
Can add new dimensions
and lift love above
The rapturous ecstasies
of 'falling in love' –
For ecstasy passes
but it is replaced
By something much greater
that cannot be defaced,
For what was 'in part'
has now 'become whole' –
For on the 'wings of the flesh,'
love entered the 'soul'!

There's Always a Springtime

After the Winter comes the Spring
To show us again that in everything
There's always renewal divinely planned,
Flawlessly perfect, the work of God's Hand . . .
And just like the seasons that come and go
When the flowers of Spring lay buried in snow,
God sends to the heart in its winter of sadness
A springtime awakening of new hope and gladness,
And loved ones who sleep in a season of death
Will, too, be awakened by God's life-giving breath.

It Takes the Bitter and the Sweet to Make a Life Full and Complete

Life is a mixture
of sunshine and rain,
Laughter and teardrops,
pleasure and pain –
Low tides and high tides,
mountains and plains,
Triumphs, defeats
and losses and gains –
But *Always* in *All Ways*
God's guiding and leading
And He alone knows
the things we're most needing –
And when He sends sorrow
or some dreaded affliction,
Be assured that it comes
with God's kind benediction –
And if we accept it
as a *Gift of His Love*,
We'll be showered with blessings
from *Our Father Above*.

Let Not Your Heart be Troubled

Whenever I am troubled
and lost in deep despair
I bundle all my troubles up
and go to God in prayer . . .

I tell Him I am heartsick
and lost and lonely, too,
That my mind is deeply burdened
and I don't know what to do . . .

But I know He stilled the tempest
and calmed the angry sea
And I humbly ask if in His love
He'll do the same for me . . .

And then I just keep *Quiet*
and think only thoughts of *Peace*
And if I abide in *Stillness*
my 'restless murmurings' cease.

Because He Lives . . .
We too Shall Live

In this restless world of struggle
it is very hard to find
Answers to the questions
that daily come to mind –
We cannot see the future,
what's beyond is still unknown,
For the secret of God's Kingdom
still belongs to Him alone –
But He granted us salvation
when His Son was crucified,
For life became immortal
because our Saviour died.

Not by Chance nor Happenstance

Into our lives come many things
to break the dull routine,
The things we had not planned on
that happen unforeseen,
The unexpected little joys
that are scattered on our way,
Success we did not count on
or a rare, fulfilling day –
A catchy, lilting melody
that makes us want to dance,
A nameless exaltation
of enchantment and romance –
An unsought word of kindness,
a compliment or two
That sets the eyes to gleaming
like crystal drops of dew –
The unplanned sudden meeting
that comes with sweet surprise
And lights the heart with happiness
like a rainbow in the skies . . .

Now some folks call it fickle fate
and some folks call it chance,
While others just accept it
as a pleasant happenstance –
But no matter what you call it,
it didn't come without design,
For all our lives are fashioned
by the *Hand That is Divine* –
And every happy happening
and every lucky break
Are little gifts from God above
that are ours to freely take.

Life is Forever!
Death is a Dream!

If we did not go to sleep at night
We'd never awaken to see the light,
And the joy of watching a new day break
Or meeting the dawn by some quiet lake
Would never be ours unless we slept
While God and all His angels kept
A vigil through this 'little death'
That's over with the morning's breath –
And death, too, is a time of sleeping,
For those who die are in God's keeping
And there's a 'sunrise' for each soul,
For *Life* not *Death* is God's promised goal –
So trust God's promise and doubt Him never
For only through death can man *Live Forever!*

Keep Our Country in Your Care

We are faced with many problems
that grow bigger day by day
And, as we seek to solve them
in our own self-sufficient way,
We keep drifting into chaos
and our avarice and greed
Blinds us to the answer
that would help us in our need . . .
Oh, God, renew our spirit
and make us more aware
That our future is dependent
on sacrifice and prayer,
Forgive us our transgressions
and revive our faith anew
So we may all draw closer
to each other and to You . . .
For when a nation is too proud
to daily kneel and pray
It will crumble into chaos
and descend into decay,
So stir us with compassion
and raise our standards higher
And take away our lust for power
and make our one desire
To be a *Shining Symbol*
of *All That's Great and Good*
As You lead us in our struggle
toward *New-Found Brotherhood!*

This I Believe

Somehow the world seems to be most deeply concerned and curiously interested in '*Who We Are.*' But '*Who We Are*' is of such small importance to *God*, for *His* deep concern is with '*What We Are.*' And complete and full knowledge of '*What We Are*' is known to *God* alone, for man's small, shallow judgments are so empty of the *Goodness* and *Greatness* of *God's Merciful Love*. And while man's motives and missions, his programmes and projects and his accomplishments and acclaim can make him successful and secure for him a listing in '*Who's Who,*' he remains *Unlisted* in *God's* '*Who's Who,*' for great is the power of might and mind . . . *But Only Love Can Make Us Kind* . . . and all we are or hope to be . . . is empty pride and vanity . . . if love is not a part of all . . . *The Greatest Man is Very Small!*

I am a very simple, uncomplicated person, and I possess only a *Child's Faith*, which completely answers all of my questions, satisfies all my longings, and never prompts me to seek a detailed explanation of how *God* works or to make a scientific study of *His* methods and *His* motives.

When I attended Sunday school, which is now much more than half a century ago, I used to sing, with all the joy that a child's heart can hold, '*Jesus Loves Me,*' for I knew *He* loved me then and that *He* would love me forever. This same knowledge still suffices to fill me with *The Same Childlike Faith I* possessed then, for I believe only a child can really know the *Greatness of God's Love*. I think that in searching and studying and using our man-made theories, we tend to destroy the *Power*, the *Glory*, the *Greatness*, and, most of all, the '*Incomprehensible Miracle*' of *God* and *His Son*.

I ask for no sensational, spectacular evidence or proof that *God* is *My Father* and that *His Son, Jesus, Loves Me*. I only know that *He* who brought me into this world will also take me safely back . . . for though there are many things I lack . . . *He* will not let me go alone . . . into a land that is unknown. And with that knowledge I can travel happily on '*The Highway to Heaven*' and always with 'hurrying feet,' for I know *God* will open 'new fields of usefulness' for me, where there are no limitations, no handicaps, and no restrictions.

My outlook on life is just the simple outlook faith provides for each one of us if we do not attempt to remake *God* into a *God of Our Own Specifications*, who meets our own selfish needs.

And never think of *God* as something apart, for *He* is really a part of our heart. *He* is not in a far-away place but only a prayer away. And just because we cannot touch *His Hand* and see *His Face* does not mean that *He* is not beside us at all times. Remember, you cannot see the air or capture it with your hand, but you can feel a gentle breeze on a sunny day or the wind's powerful blast in the fury of the storm, and you know without breathing this air you would die, for, like *God*, it is truly '*The Breath of Life*.'

I just know everything that has ever happened in my life, whether it was good or bad, glad or sad, *God* sent it for a reason, and I truly believe with all my heart that '*God Never Makes Mistakes*.' I never question what *God* sends, for I realize, when you question *God*, you lose the *Unquestionable Power of Faith* and you no longer can enjoy its endless benefits.

I pray constantly, not always on my knees or at special places or at special times, nor do I use impressive words. I just keep up a running conversation with *God*, hour by hour and day by day. I talk to *Him* about everything, I ask *Him* for nothing, except the joy of knowing *Him* better and loving *Him* more.

I am not 'ritualistically religious' or 'denominationally directed,' and when columnists question me, I just answer this quote from one of my poems:

> 'Ask me not my race or creed . . . just take me in my hour of need . . . and let me know *You* love me, too . . . and that I am a part of *You* . . . for in *The Holy Father's Sight* . . . no man is yellow, black, or white.'

And I feel that every man has a deep 'heart need' that cannot be filled with doctrine or creed, for the soul of man knows nothing more than just that he is longing for a haven that is safe and sure and a fortress where he feels secure.

It is true my poems have had phenomenal sales wherever they have been made available. They are read by all creeds, all classes, all colours, all ages, and in all countries, and the people who read my writings identify with them because *God* is really a part of every heart in the world and *It is God Talking* and not me.

I never think of myself as a success or as an author or a poet. I only think of myself as another 'worker' in '*God's Vineyard*.' The phenomenal sale of my books and writings is not due to anything special about me or my way of living. It is just because people all over the world, under *God's Direction*, have seen their own souls reflected in the words I have borrowed from *God*.

When people write, telephone, or cable to come and see

me, I strongly discourage them, because they do not realize that in meeting me, they are just meeting themselves, for the same *God* who abides in them abides in me and *He* reaches from heart to heart. *Time* and *Space* mean nothing when *God Takes Over*, for all physical and material limitations fade before the *Power* of *Spiritual Reality*.

All my verses are 'woven' from 'the silken strands of thought' provided in the letters I receive and the conversations I have with people. For no matter how we mask our feelings outwardly, we all at some time experience the same many-faceted emotions that come to all mankind, often unwelcomed, unsought, unwanted, and unheralded, and no matter how adept man is at disguising what he really is inside, we all do share these same human emotions. We are all lonely, but we are never alone . . . for *God* is our *Father* and we are *His Own* . . . we are all subject to trials and tribulation . . . but we are always welcome to seek *God* in meditation . . . we are all disappointed and have hours of despair . . . but we always have access to our *Father* in prayer . . . and all we ever have to do is to '*Let Go and Let God!*'

All our troubles and problems, as individuals or as a nation, stem from our incurable, unconquerable curiosity and our grim determination to find out '*Who*' or '*What*' *Created Creation* and we all aspire to find out '*Who God Really Is.*' We are constantly seeking and searching for *New Ways* to solve *Old Problems* without giving *Faith* a real chance. We have *Faith*, but we do not have *Enough Faith*, and man cannot bring himself to 'lose himself in the *Love* of *God*.'

All these '*Olden Golden Truths*' that are constantly repeated through the ages just substantiate the *Majestic Truth of Ecclesiastes*, for '*There is Nothing New Under The Sun.*' Everything that has been before will be again, for as long as there are selfish, greedy, arrogant men who think

46

they can outmanœuvre, outguess, outdo, and outmanipulate *God*, they will never find the solution to the problems on earth. So, the *Seasons* come and the *Seasons* go . . . and the *Rivers* flow and the *Winds* still blow . . . and *God* still smiles and watches man . . . knowing always '*Man Can't* but *He Can!*'

I am well aware that I cannot make it on my own, and I ask *God* to take my hand and hold it tight, for I cannot walk alone. Each day *God* only asks us to do our best, and then *He* will take over and do all the rest. And remember, *God* is always available and ready to help anyone who asks *Him*, for *God* is *Here* . . . *He's There* . . . *He's Everywhere* . . . *He's* as close to you as *He* is to me . . . and wherever you are *God* is sure to be. And I want you to know that the poems I write are not mine alone . . . they belong to *God* and to the people I've known . . . and while I may never have met you face-to-face . . . in *God's Love* and by *His Grace* . . . our hearts and mind can meet and share . . . my little poems of *Faith* and *Prayer* . . . and though we are oceans and miles apart . . . *God* unites us in *Spirit* and *Heart!*

A Word from the Author
'Just For You'

My heart rejoices and I'm thankful, too,
That I could share this book with you
For this book is truly a *'Gift of Love'*
For all my poems are woven of
Words I borrow from Our Father Above
For this is a *'Partnership of Three,'*
God First, then *You*, and last of all *Me* . . .
For I'm not an author writing for fame
Seeking new laurels or praise for my name,
I am only a 'worker' employed by the Lord
And great is my gladness and rich my reward
If I can just spread the wonderful story
That *God* is the *Answer* to *Eternal*
Glory . . .
And only the people who read my poems
Can help me to reach more *Hearts* and *Homes*,
Bringing new hope and comfort and cheer,
Telling sad hearts there is nothing to fear
And what greater joy could there be than to share
The *Love* of *God* and the *Power* of *Prayer*!

May *God's Love* and *His Joy* flow around this troubled
world and may *You* and I together help to make this a
Reality. This is the wish and the prayer of